MW00817563

25 CHRISTMAS
DUETS

COMPILED AND ARRANGED BY
BRYCE INMAN

DESIGN BY
STUDIO122

© 2003 Word Music, a division of Word Music Group, LLC.
All Rights Reserved. International Copyright Secured. Printed in U.S.A.

No part of this publication may be reproduced or transmitted in any form or by any means, electronic or mechanical, including
photocopy, recording or any information storage and retrieval system, without permission in writing from the publisher.

CONTENTS

Possession of a CCLI license does not give you permission to make any copy of the music contained in this book. If you are unsure as to what rights you do have to copy under a CCLI license or if you want information about CCLI, please call 1-800-234-2446.

BREATH OF HEAVEN (MARY'S SONG)

Recorded by Amy Grant

Words and Music by
CHRIS EATON
and AMY GRANT
Vocal arrangement by Bryce Inman

Slowly, with reflection

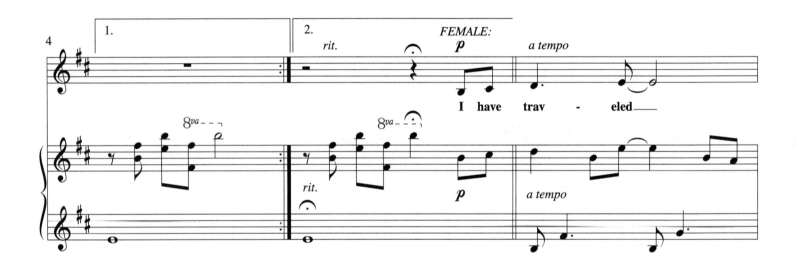

© Copyright 1992 Bug Music o/b/o SGO Music Publishing Ltd./Age to Age Music, Inc. (adm. by The Loving Company)
All Rights Reserved. Used by Permission.

EVEN IF YOU POSSESS A **CCLI** LICENSE YOU CANNOT COPY ANY MUSIC FROM THIS BOOK.
If you have questions about CCLI, please call 800/234-2446.

Mary, Did You Know?

Recorded by Michael English

Words and Music by
MARK LOWRY
and BUDDY GREENE
Vocal arrangement by Bryce Inman

1. Ma - ry, did you

© Copyright 1991 Word Music, LLC/
Rufus Music (adm. by Gaither Copyright Management)
All Rights Reserved. Used by Permission.

EVEN IF YOU POSSESS A **CCLI** LICENSE YOU CANNOT COPY ANY MUSIC FROM THIS BOOK.
If you have questions about CCLI, please call 800/234-2446.

It's Christmas Time

Recorded by City on a Hill

Words and Music by
TERRY SCOTT TAYLOR
and STEVE HINDALONG
Vocal arrangement by Bryce Inman

© Copyright 2002 Zoom Daddy Music/New Spring Publishing, Inc./
Never Say Never Songs (both adm. by Brentwood-Benson Music Publishing, Inc.)
All Rights Reserved. Used by Permission.

EVEN IF YOU POSSESS A **CCLI** LICENSE YOU CANNOT COPY ANY MUSIC FROM THIS BOOK.
If you have questions about CCLI, please call 800/234-2446.

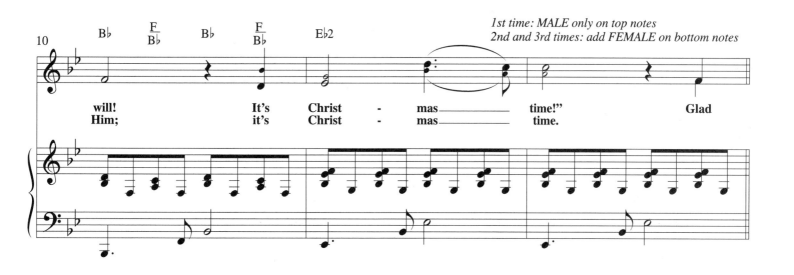

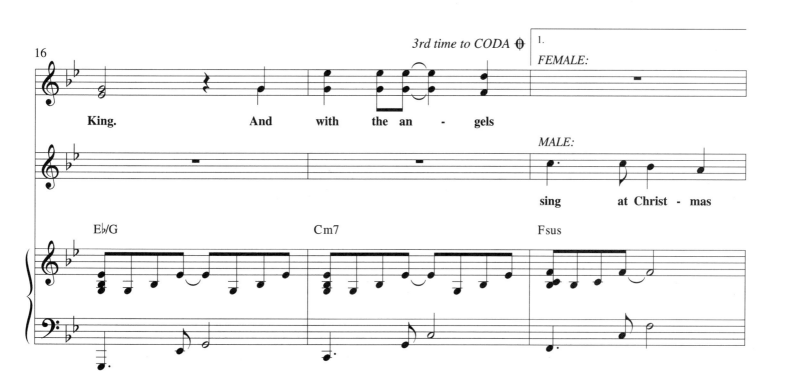

Don't Save It All for Christmas Day

Recorded by Avalon

**Words and Music by
PETER ZIZZO, RIC WAKE
and CELINE DION**
Vocal arrangement by Bryce Inman

© Copyright 1998 Make It Rock Publishing/Annotation Music/
Duffield Music/Connotation Music/Pez Music
All rights on behalf of Make It Rock Publishing and Annotation Music adm. by WB Music Corp.
All rights on behalf of Duffield Corp. adm. by Sony/ATV Music Publishing, 8 Music Square West, Nashville, TN 37203.
All rights on behalf of Connotation Music and Pez Music adm. by Warner-Tamerlane Publishing Corp.
All Rights Reserved. Used by Permission.

EVEN IF YOU POSSESS A **CCLI** LICENSE YOU CANNOT COPY ANY MUSIC FROM THIS BOOK.
If you have questions about CCLI, please call 800/234-2446.

A Prayer for Every Year
based on "Grown-up Christmas List"
Recorded by Plus One

Words and Music by
DAVID FOSTER and
LINDA THOMPSON
Vocal arrangement by Bryce Inman

With much feeling ♩ = 60

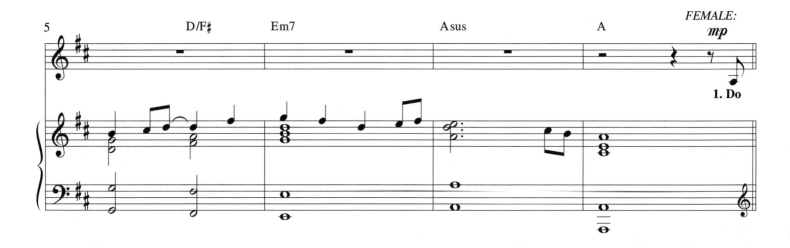

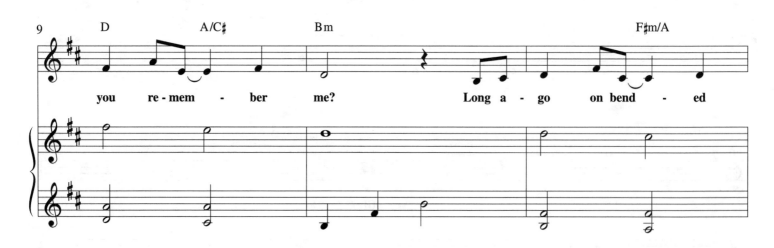

you re - mem - ber me? Long a - go on bend - ed

© Copyright 1992 Air Bear Music (adm. by Peermusic Ltd.)/Warner Tamerlane Publishing Corp./
Brandon Brody Music (adm. by Warner-Tamerlane Publishing Corp.)
All Rights Reserved. Used by Permission.

EVEN IF YOU POSSESS A **CCLI** LICENSE YOU CANNOT COPY ANY MUSIC FROM THIS BOOK.
If you have questions about CCLI, please call 800/234-2446.

The Angel Song

Recorded by Jaci Velasquez

**Words and Music by
CHRIS EATON**
Vocal arrangement by Bryce Inman

© Copyright 2001 Dayspring Music, LLC/SGO Music Publishing, Ltd. (adm. by Dayspring Music, LLC)
All Rights Reserved. Used by Permission.

EVEN IF YOU POSSESS A **CCLI** LICENSE YOU CANNOT COPY ANY MUSIC FROM THIS BOOK.
If you have questions about CCLI, please call 800/234-2446.

As I gaze in - to sun - sets, o - ver sil - hou - ette moun -

- tains, ____ I am a - mazed ____ that the God who made

all ____ this, made me. ____

MALE:

FEMALE: melody

2. As

44

Not That Far from Bethlehem

Recorded by Point of Grace

Words and Music by
JEFF BORDERS, GAYLA BORDERS
and LOWELL ALEXANDER
Vocal arrangement by Bryce Inman

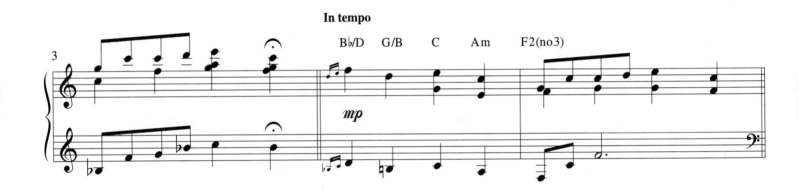

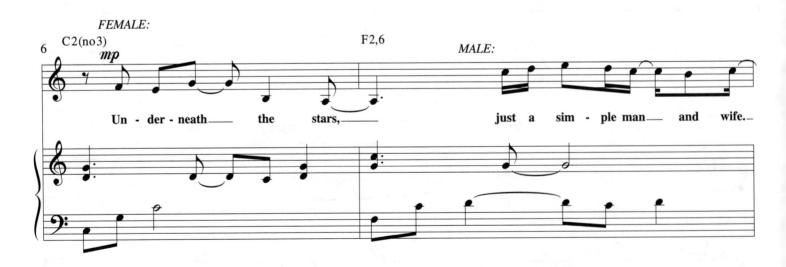

Underneath the stars, just a simple man and wife.

© Copyright 1999 Sony/ATV Tunes LLC/Sony /ATV Songs LLC/Randy Cox Music, Inc./Grayson Castle Songs
All rights on behalf of Sony/ATV Tunes LLC, Sony/ATV Songs LLC and Grayson Castle Songs adm. by
Sony/ATV Music Pub., 8 Music Square West, Nashville, TN 37203
All Rights Reserved. Used by Permission.

EVEN IF YOU POSSESS A CCLI LICENSE YOU CANNOT COPY ANY MUSIC FROM THIS BOOK.
If you have questions about CCLI, please call 800/234-2446.

LIGHT OF THE STABLE

Recorded by Selah.

**Words and Music by
STEVE RHYMER and
ELIZABETH RHYMER**
Vocal arrangement by Bryce Inman

With a strong beat ♩ = 108

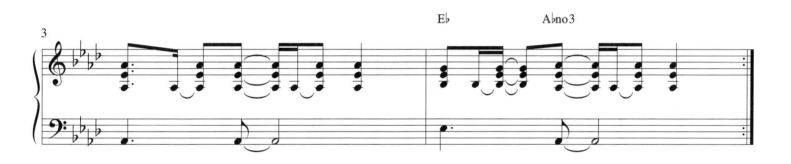

© Copyright 1975 Tessa Publishing Company (adm. by MCS Music America, Inc.)
All Rights Reserved. Used by Permission.

EVEN IF YOU POSSESS A **CCLI** LICENSE YOU CANNOT COPY ANY MUSIC FROM THIS BOOK.
If you have questions about CCLI, please call 800/234-2446.

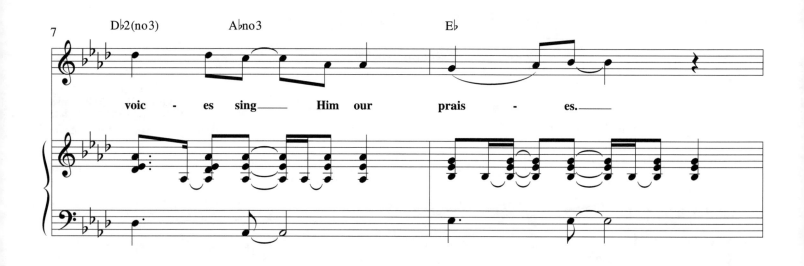

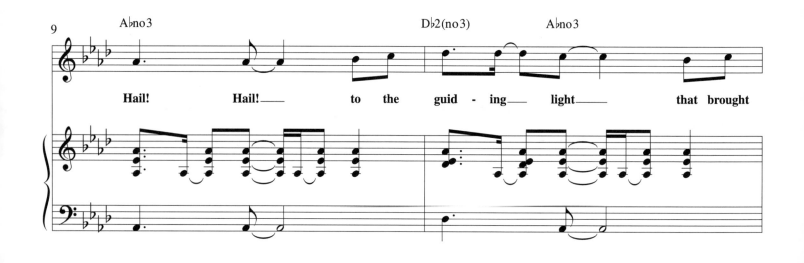

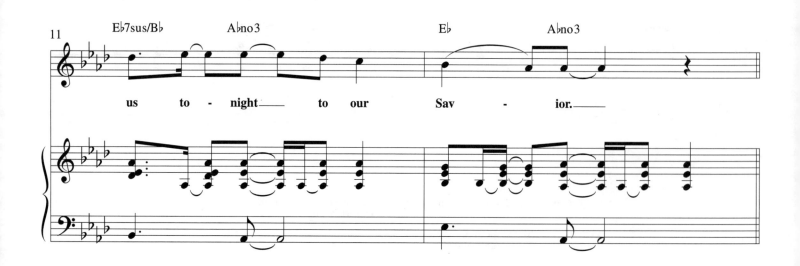

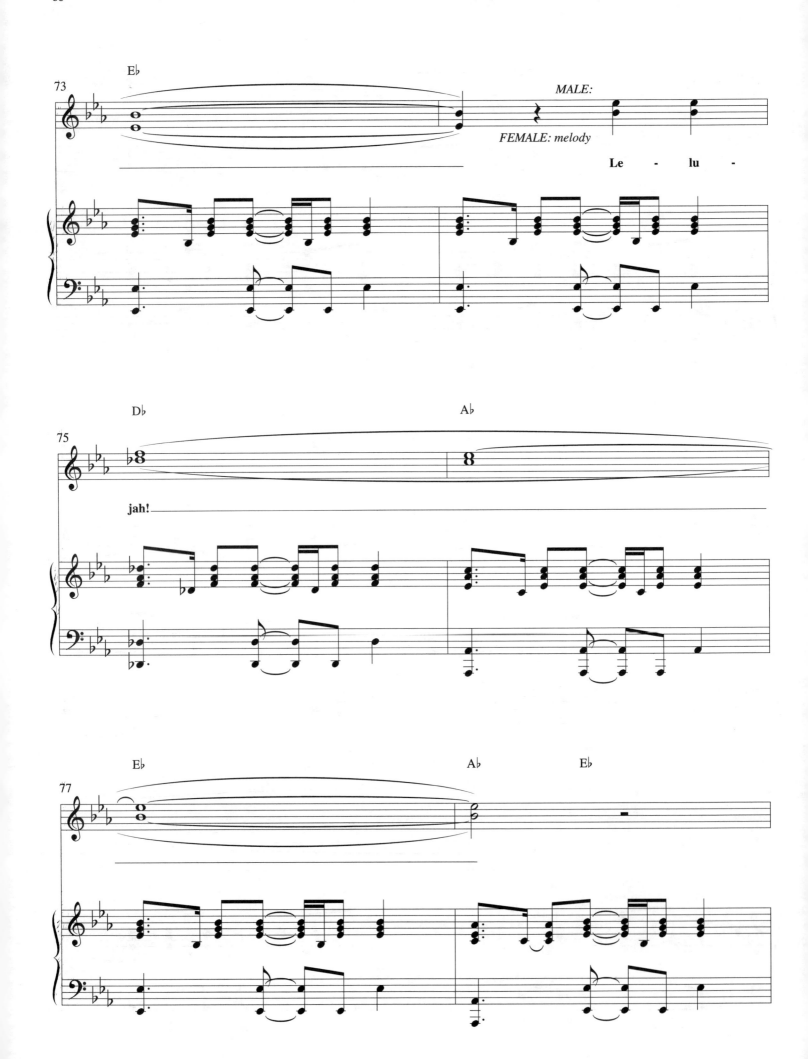

Hail! Hail!_____ to the new - born___ King!_____

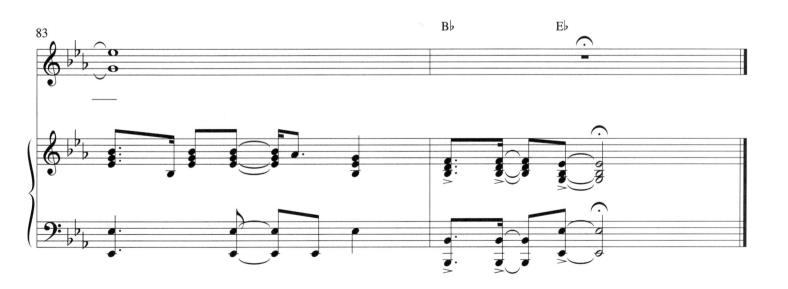

Lamb of God

Recorded by Nicole C. Mullen

Words and Music by
NICOLE C. MULLEN
and DAVID MULLEN
Vocal arrangement by Bryce Inman

© Copyright 2002 Wordspring Music, LLC/Lil' Jas' Music (adm. by Wordspring Music, LLC)/
Funkabilly Music/Who's JO (adm. by JO Music Services, LLC)
All Rights Reserved. Used by Permission.

EVEN IF YOU POSSESS A **CCLI** LICENSE YOU CANNOT COPY ANY MUSIC FROM THIS BOOK.
If you have questions about CCLI, please call 800/234-2446.

(from "O Come, All Ye Faithful" - Latin Hymn; John Francis Wade)

Silent Night

Recorded by Mark Schultz and Nichole Nordeman

JOSEPH MOHR

FRANZ GRÜBER
Arranged by Peter Kipley
Vocal arrangement by Bryce Inman

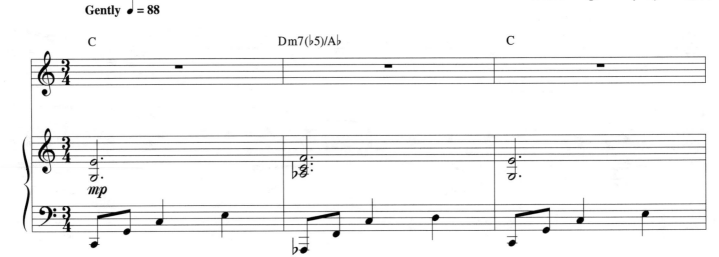

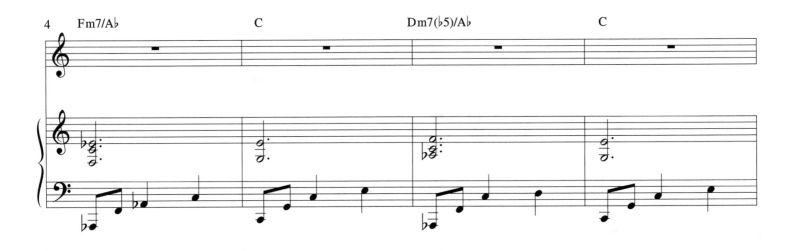

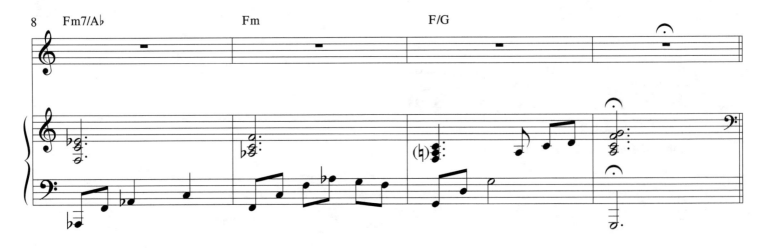

Arr. © Copyright 2002 Wordspring Music, LLC/Songs From The Indigo Room (adm. by Wordspring Music, LLC)
All Rights Reserved. Used by Permission.

EVEN IF YOU POSSESS A **CCLI** LICENSE YOU CANNOT COPY ANY MUSIC FROM THIS BOOK.
If you have questions about CCLI, please call 800/234-2446.

CHILD OF LOVE

Recorded by Sara Groves

Words and Music by
MATTHEW WEST, STEVE HINDALONG
and MARK LEE
Vocal arrangement by Bryce Inman

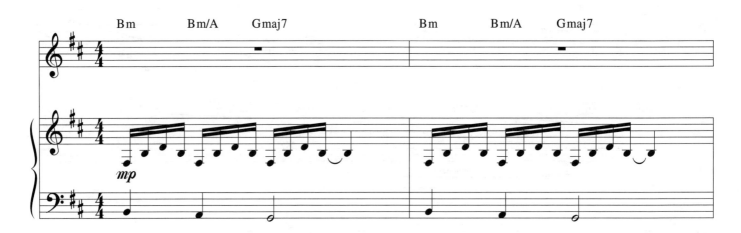

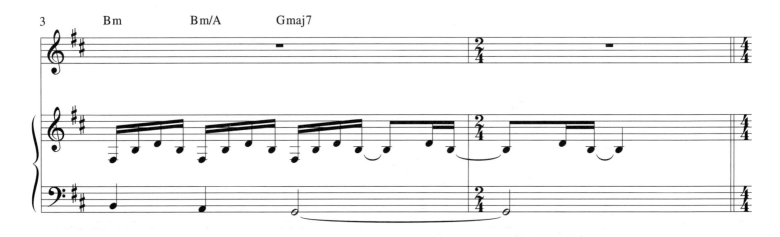

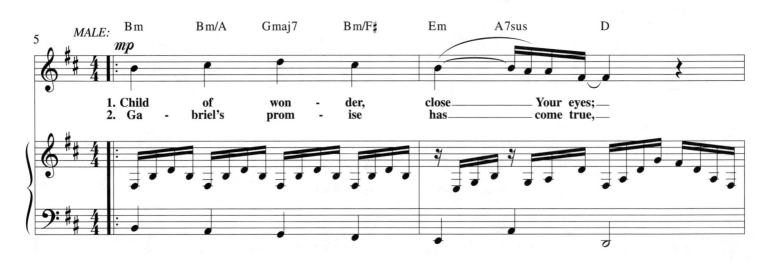

1. Child of won - der, close Your eyes;
2. Ga - briel's prom - ise has come true,

© Copyright 2002 Word Music, LLC/New Spring Publishing, Inc./
Never Say Never Songs (both adm. by Brentwood-Benson Music Publishing, Inc.)
All Rights Reserved. Used by Permission.

EVEN IF YOU POSSESS A **CCLI** LICENSE YOU CANNOT COPY ANY MUSIC FROM THIS BOOK.
If you have questions about CCLI, please call 800/234-2446.

CHRISTMASTIME

Recorded by Michael W. Smith

**Words and Music by
MICHAEL W. SMITH
and JOANNA CARLSON**
Vocal arrangement by Bryce Inman

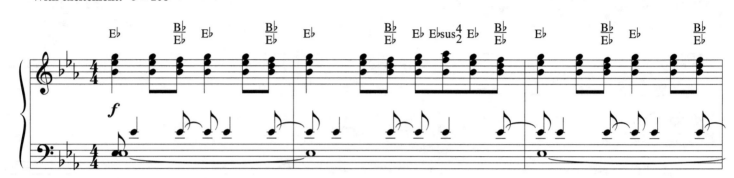

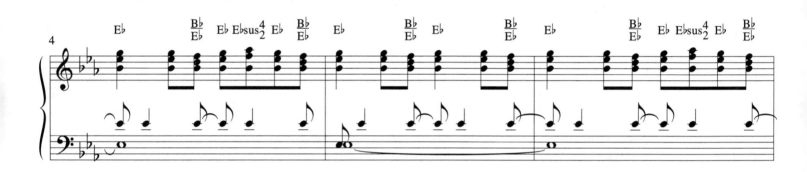

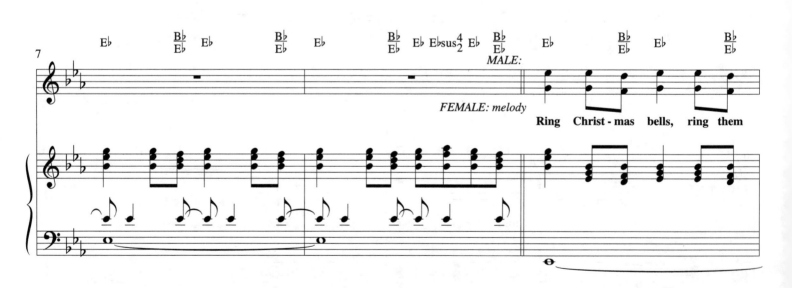

© Copyright 1998 Sony/ATV Tunes LLC/Deer Valley Music/Lil' Yella House Music (adm. by Dayspring Music, LLC)/Dayspring Music, LLC
All rights for Sony/ATV Tunes LLC and Deer Valley Music adm. by Sony/ATV Music Publishing, 8 Music Square West, Nashville, TN 37203
All Rights Reserved. Used by Permission.

EVEN IF YOU POSSESS A **CCLI** LICENSE, YOU CANNOT COPY ANY MUSIC FROM THIS BOOK.
If you have questions about CCLI, please call 800/234-2446.

We Are the Reason

Recorded by Avalon

Words and Music by
DAVID MEECE
Vocal arrangement by Bryce Inman

Slow four ♩ = 60

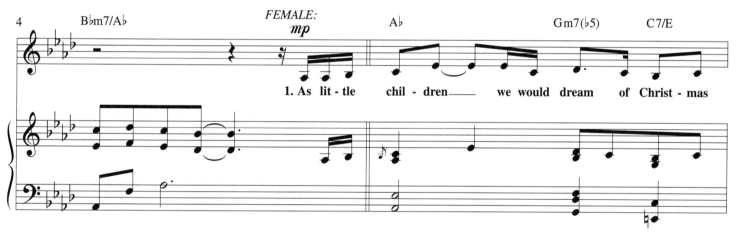

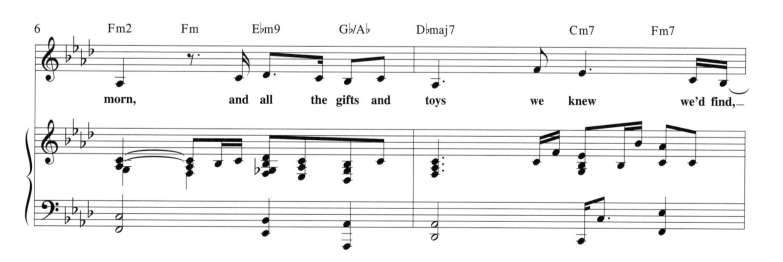

© Copyright 1980 Word Music, LLC
All Rights Reserved. Used by Permission.

EVEN IF YOU POSSESS A **CCLI** LICENSE YOU CANNOT COPY ANY MUSIC FROM THIS BOOK.
If you have questions about CCLI, please call 800/234-2446.

The Gift

Recorded by Randy Travis

Words and Music by
PHILLIP MOORE
and RAY SCOTT
Vocal arrangement by Bryce Inman

Moderately ♩ = 69

1. He was born in Beth - le - hem, _____ they _____ say. There was a

star to light _____ the path _____ to where He _____ lay.

© Copyright 2002 Green Dogg Music, Inc.
All Rights Reserved. Used by Permission.

EVEN IF YOU POSSESS A **CCLI** LICENSE YOU CANNOT COPY ANY MUSIC FROM THIS BOOK.
If you have questions about CCLI, please call 800/234-2446.

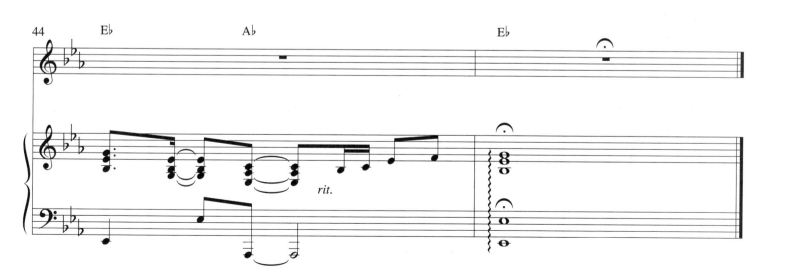

Sent by the Father

Recorded by Ray Boltz

Words and Music by
RAY BOLTZ and
STEVE MILLIKAN
Vocal arrangement by Bryce Inman

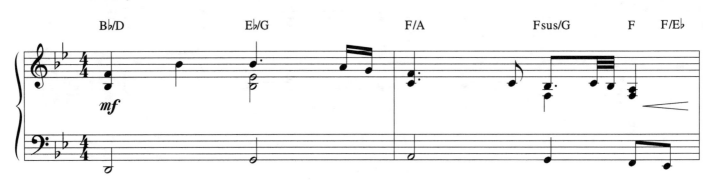

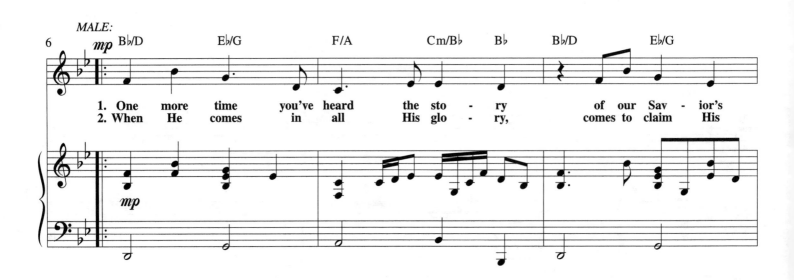

1. One more time you've heard the sto-ry of our Sav-ior's
2. When He comes in all His glo-ry, comes to claim His

© Copyright 1998 Shepherd Boy Music (adm. by Word Music, LLC)/Weedom & Reap
All Rights Reserved. Used by Permission.

EVEN IF YOU POSSESS A **CCLI** LICENSE YOU CANNOT COPY ANY MUSIC FROM THIS BOOK.
If you have questions about CCLI, please call 800/234-2446.

This Gift

Recorded by Point of Grace

**Words and Music by
STEVE AMERSON and
DAVID T. CLYDESDALE**
Vocal arrangement by Bryce Inman

© Copyright 1994 Word Music, LLC/Dayspring Music, LLC
All Rights Reserved. Used by Permission.

EVEN IF YOU POSSESS A **CCLI** LICENSE YOU CANNOT COPY ANY MUSIC FROM THIS BOOK.
If you have questions about CCLI, please call 800/234-2446.

Christmas Lullaby
(I Will Lead You Home)

Recorded by Amy Grant

Words and Music by
AMY GRANT
and CHRIS EATON
Vocal arrangement by Bryce Inman

Sweetly ♩ = 88

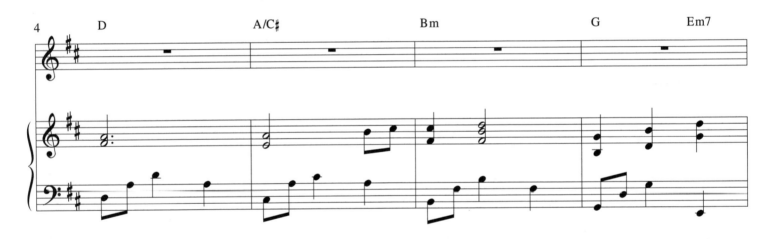

1. Are you far a-way from home this
(2. How) beau-ti-ful, how pre-cious the

© Copyright 1999 Grant Girls Music, Inc. (adm. by The Loving Co.)/
Dayspring Music, LLC/SGO Music Publishing, Ltd. (adm. by Dayspring Music, LLC)
All Rights Reserved. Used by Permission.

EVEN IF YOU POSSESS A **CCLI** LICENSE YOU CANNOT COPY ANY MUSIC FROM THIS BOOK.
If you have questions about CCLI, please call 800/234-2446.

How gent - ly, how ten - der - ly He says to one and all,

verse from "Away in a Manger" by John T. McFarland

Sing Noel

Recorded by Newsong

Words and Music by
MICHAEL O'BRIEN
and EDDIE CARSWELL
Vocal arrangement by Bryce Inman

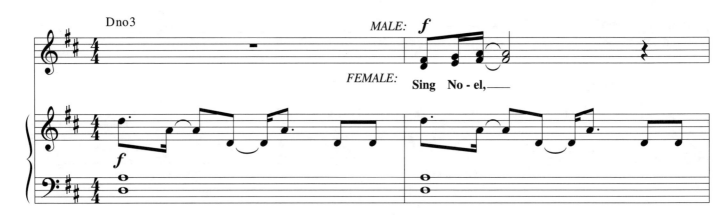

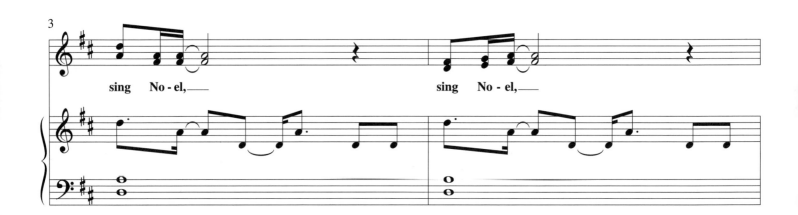

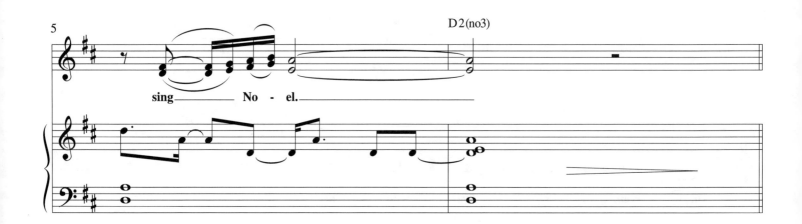

© Copyright 2002 Bridge Building Music, Inc./Sheltering Tree Music/Designer Music Group, Inc.
(All rights adm. by Brentwood-Benson Music Publishing, Inc.)
All Rights Reserved. Used by Permission.

EVEN IF YOU POSSESS A **CCLI** LICENSE YOU CANNOT COPY ANY MUSIC FROM THIS BOOK.
If you have questions about CCLI, please call 800/234-2446.

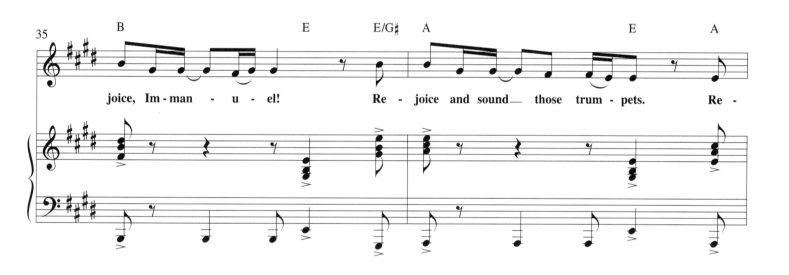

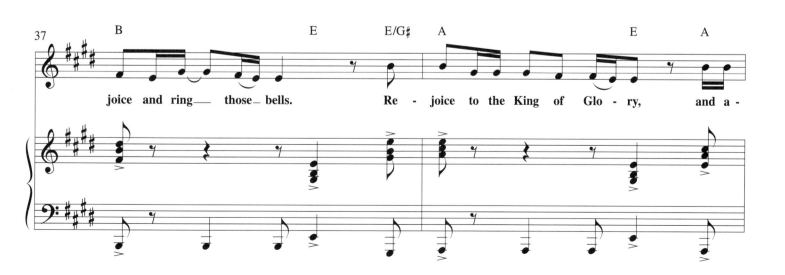

O Holy Night!

Recorded by Point of Grace

JOHN S. DWIGHT

ADOLPHE ADAM
Arranged by Carl Marsh
Vocal arrangement by Bryce Inman

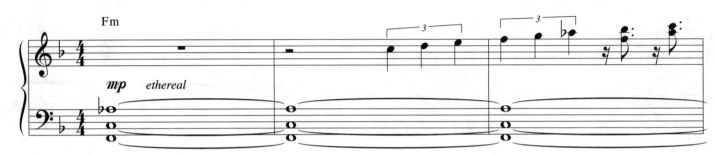

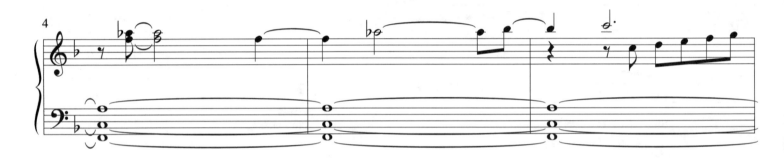

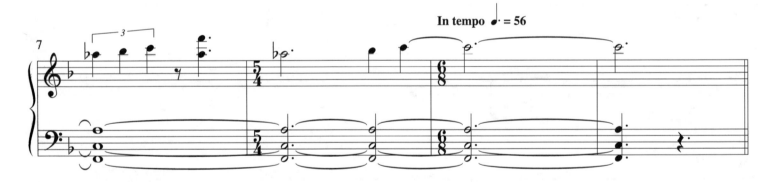

Arr. © Copyright 1993 Little Discoveries
All rights controlled and adm. by Mosaic Music Publishing, LLC
All Rights Reserved. Used by Permission.

EVEN IF YOU POSSESS A **CCLI** LICENSE YOU CANNOT COPY ANY MUSIC FROM THIS BOOK.
If you have questions about CCLI, please call 800/234-2446.

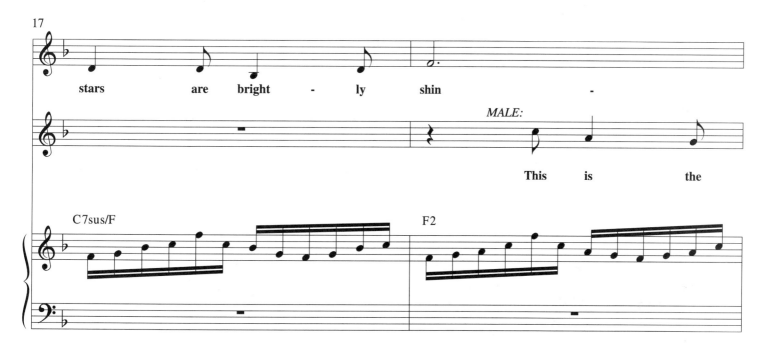

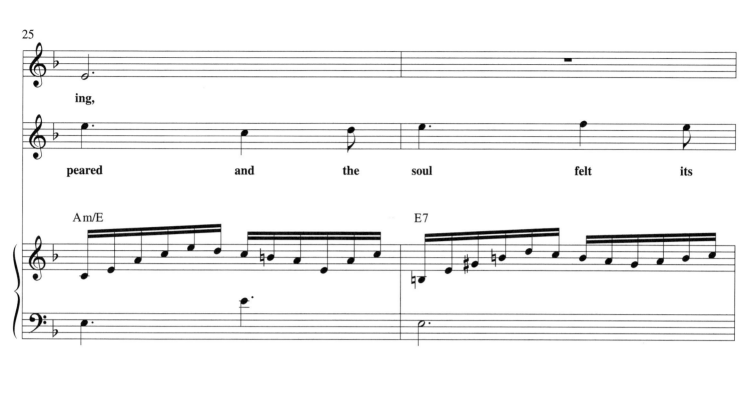

ing,

peared   and   the   soul   felt   its

BOTH:

worth.

A

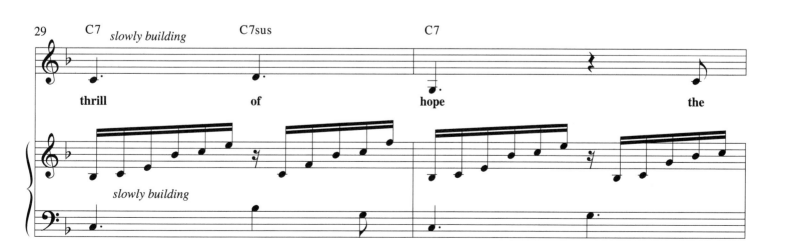

thrill   of   hope   the

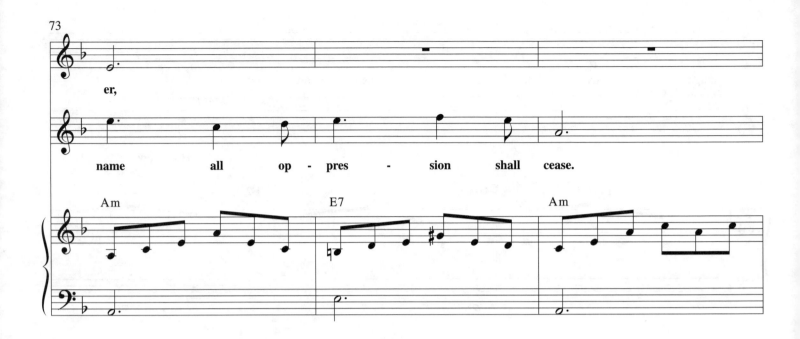

er,

name all op - pres - sion shall cease.

BOTH:

Sweet hymns of joy in

grate - ful cho - rus raise we, Let all with -

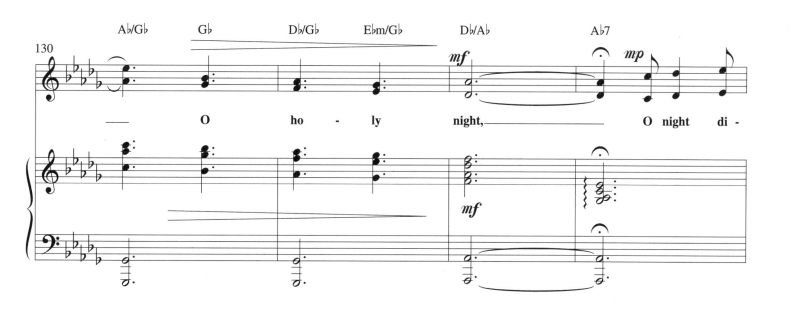

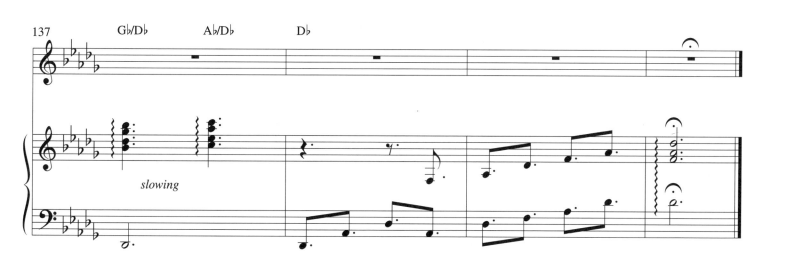

Merry Christmas, Baby

Recorded by Nicole C. Mullen

Words and Music by
NICOLE C. MULLEN
Vocal arrangement by Bryce Inman

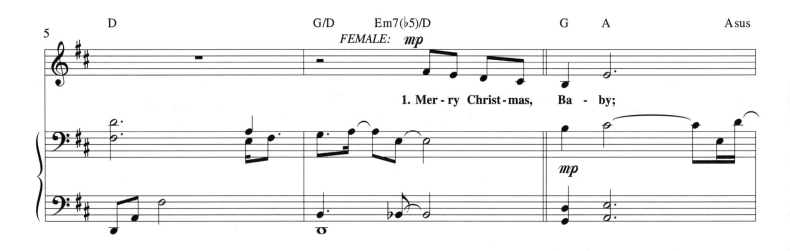

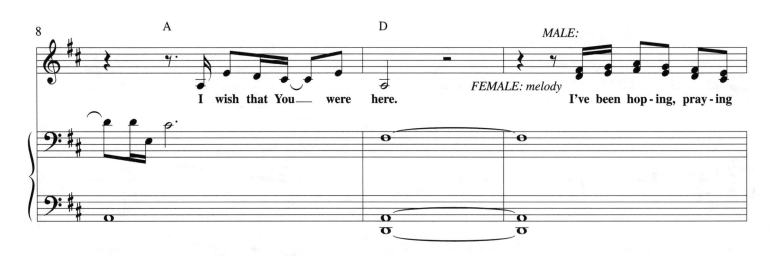

© Copyright 2002 Wordspring Music, LLC/Lil' Jas' Music (adm. by Wordspring Music, LLC)
All Rights Reserved. Used by Permission.

EVEN IF YOU POSSESS A **CCLI** LICENSE YOU CANNOT COPY ANY MUSIC FROM THIS BOOK.
If you have questions about CCLI, please call 800/234-2446.

A Strange Way to Save the World

Recorded by 4HIM

**Words and Music by
DAVE CLARK, MARK HARRIS
and DON KOCH**
Vocal arrangement by Bryce Inman

Steady four ♩ = 116

1. I'm sure he must have been sur-prised—
(2. To think of how it) could have been—

MALE:

add FEMALE on cued harmony 2nd time

© Copyright 1993 John T. Benson Publishing/First Verse Music/Paragon Music Corp./
Point Clear Music (all adm. by Brentwood-Benson Music Publishing, Inc.)/A-Knack-For-This Music (adm. by ICG)
All Rights Reserved. Used by Permission.

EVEN IF YOU POSSESS A **CCLI** LICENSE YOU CANNOT COPY ANY MUSIC FROM THIS BOOK.
If you have questions about CCLI, please call 800/234-2446.æ

Season of Love

Recorded by Jaci Velasquez

**Words and Music by
GEORGE COCCHINI, HUNTER DAVIS
and CHRIS FAULK**
Vocal arrangement by Bryce Inman

Moderate ballad ♩ = 116

© Copyright 2001 Topboost Music (adm. by Moon & Musky Music)/Jax & Broder Music/
Pelican Lips Music (both adm. by ION Music Administration)/Deston Songs/Boat Money Music
All rights on behalf of Deston Songs and Boat Money Music adm. by Sony/ATV Music Publishing,
8 Music Square West, Nashville, TN 37203
All Rights Reserved. Used by Permission.

EVEN IF YOU POSSESS A **CCLI** LICENSE YOU CANNOT COPY ANY MUSIC FROM THIS BOOK.
If you have questions about CCLI, please call 800/234-2446.

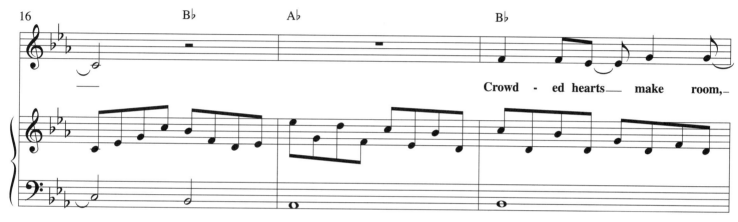

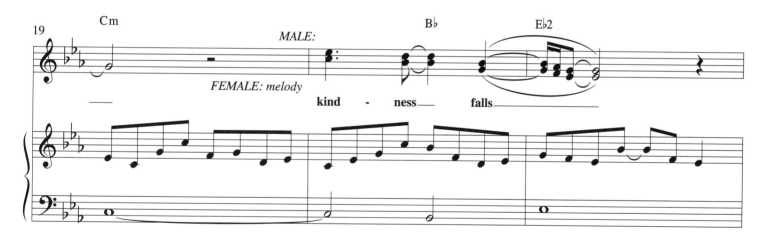

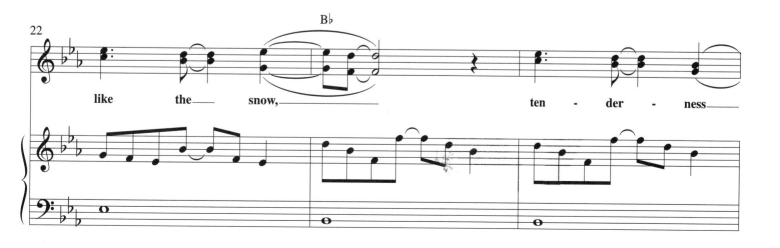

our — hands.

MALE:
Sea - son — of love, — in the dark - ness, to be — hope, to give — joy;

MALE: melody

FEMALE:
all o - ver the world, — it's Christ - mas. Sea - son — of

LIGHT A CANDLE

Recorded by Avalon

Words and Music by
JOEL LINDSEY
and WAYNE HAUN
Vocal arrangement by Bryce Inman

Slow four ♩ = 76

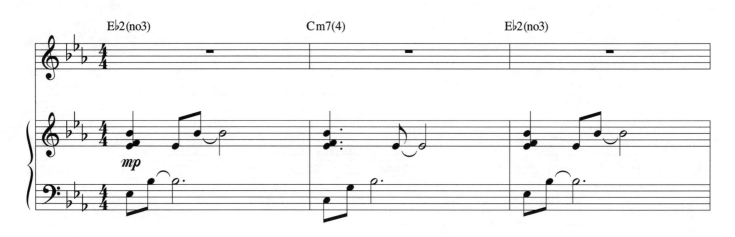

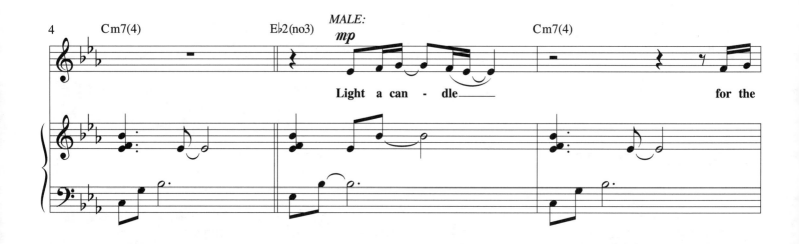

Light a can - dle _____ for the

old man who sits star - ing out a frost - y ___ win - dow - pane;

© Copyright 2000 Paragon Music Corp./Vacation Boy Music (adm. by Brentwood-Benson Music Publishing, Inc.)/
Christian Taylor Music (a div. of Daywind Music Publishing)
All Rights Reserved. Used by Permission.

EVEN IF YOU POSSESS A CCLI LICENSE YOU CANNOT COPY ANY MUSIC FROM THIS BOOK.
If you have questions about CCLI, please call 800/234-2446.

When Love Came Down

Recorded by Point of Grace

Words and Music by
CHRIS EATON
Vocal arrangement by Bryce Inman

With excitement ♩ = 112

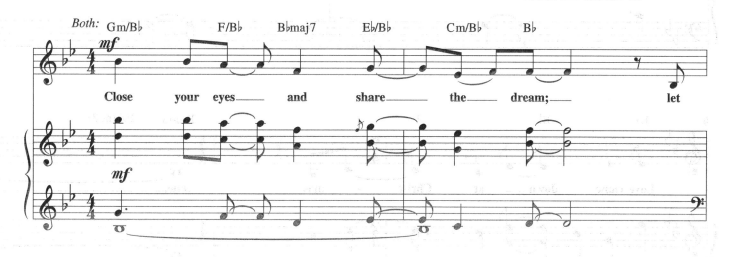

© Copyright 1999 Bug Music o/b/o SGO Music Publishing Ltd.
All Rights Reserved. Used by Permission.

EVEN IF YOU POSSESS A CCLI LICENSE YOU CANNOT COPY ANY MUSIC FROM THIS BOOK.
If you have questions about CCLI, please call 800/234-2446.

Welcome to Our World

Recorded by Chris Rice

Words and Music by
CHRIS RICE
Vocal arrangement by Bryce Inman

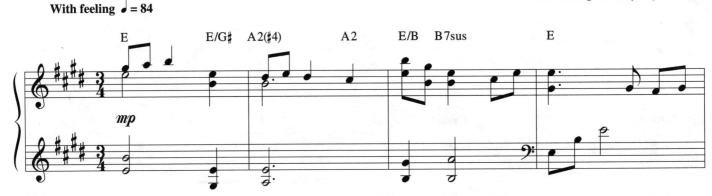

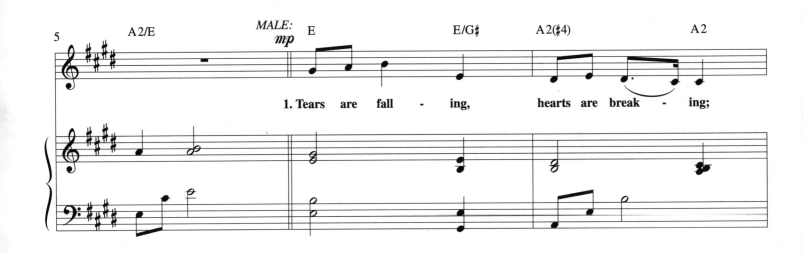

1. Tears are fall - ing, hearts are break - ing;

how we need to hear— from God. You've been prom - ised,

© Copyright 1995 Clumsy Fly Music (adm. by Word Music, LLC)
All Rights Reserved. Used by Permission.

EVEN IF YOU POSSESS A **CCLI** LICENSE YOU CANNOT COPY ANY MUSIC FROM THIS BOOK.
If you have questions about CCLI, please call 800/234-2446